The No-Sex
▮▮▮▮▮▮ HANDBOOK ▮▮▮▮▮▮

Pamela Pettler & Amy Heckerling

Illustrated by Jack Ziegler

WARNER BOOKS

A Warner Communications Company

Warner Books, Inc., 666 Fifth Avenue, New York, NY 10103

w A Warner Communications Company

Printed in the United States of America
First Printing: February 1990
10 9 8 7 6 5 4 3

Library of Congress Cataloging-in-Publication Data

Pettler, Pamela.
   The no-sex handbook / by Pamela Pettler and Amy Heckerling.
      p.   cm.
   ISBN 0-446-39054-2
   1. Sexual abstinence—Humor. 2. Sex—Humor. 3. Intimacy
(Psychology)—Humor.   I. Heckerling, Amy.   II. Title.
PN6231.S54P44   1990   89-39439
818'.5402—dc20   CIP

Book Design by Giorgetta Bell McRee

Contents

**PART SIX: IF ALL ELSE FAILS, HOW TO RUIN A
   RELATIONSHIP   79**

Conclusion   91

Introduction

ZERO SEX—THE FINAL TABOO

Zero sex. Go ahead. Say it.

How long have you secretly wondered about this hidden garden of delight, this forbidden fruit, the love that dare not even write its name? Perhaps you have looked at your friends, colleagues, and softball teammates, and suspected that surely some of them must be practicing it. Certainly so many of them seem to manage, with such effortless consistency, to destroy relationships, botch dates (if they ever get them to begin with), and repeatedly pulverize pretty much any encounter they might unaccountably have with the opposite sex.

How do they do it?

Few people are willing to share their secret techniques—if they are willing to admit to them at all. Even today, "zero sex" is not considered a topic fit for polite society. Most people find out about it on the street, that notorious breeding ground of myth and misinformation. Even your most intimate friends probably stutter embarrassedly when asked about their own lack of sex.

But it's nothing to be embarrassed about. Many, many people, far more than you might imagine, have zero sex. A few lucky souls are even able to sustain it for prolonged periods ("multiple" zero sex, as it is commonly known). And the truth is, you too can easily experience the hidden pleasures beyond this final frontier—the extra time, the extra energy, the freedom from aggravation, the new-found ability to catch up on Saturday night TV, the extra room in your bed, not to mention saving all that needless wear and tear on your underwear.

Contrary to popular belief, achieving zero sex is not that difficult. You may be thinking, "Sure, I'm not having sex now, but how can I continue?" Don't worry! In this book, we show you, clearly and straightforwardly, how not to have sex: how to avoid any sort of social opportunities—destroy them, even; how to lay waste to any sort of human interaction; how to bring any unexpected date to a swift, ruinous close—or, if you prefer, a painful, lingering close; and above all, not merely how to *avoid* sex—but, for the first time, *how to not enjoy it if you accidentally find yourself having it!* (See p. 64, "Avoiding Orgasm: Yes, You Can!")

Yes, you too can enjoy the sex-free lifestyle you've always known you were capable of. Complete "zero sex" can be yours in just a few easy lessons!

THE "ZERO-SEX" PHILOSOPHY

Why have sex?

Sure, you can point to attractive women in restaurants and say, "Yeah, I had her," but so what? Can you sell her, trade her, use her as leverage in a hostile takeover, put her in a cellar and wait for her to go up in value, wear her with your new gabardine slacks, or install a cellular phone in her?

Likewise, women can point to high-powered executives, handsome waiters, or muscular busboys and shrug acquisitively, impressing their friends, but in fact all you've done is waste anywhere from sixty down to two minutes

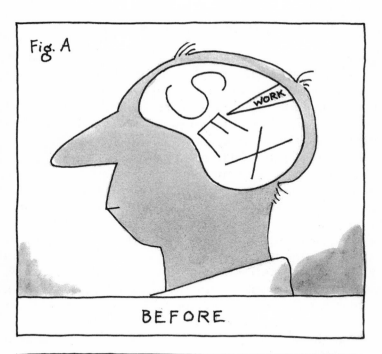

Fig. A

BEFORE

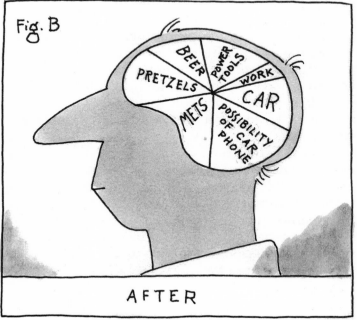

Fig. B

AFTER

(depending on whether you were sleeping with the busboy or the executive). Just think of all the things you could have accomplished! An aerobics class, a power lunch, picking up those fabulous new Maud Frizons on sale at Bergdorf's, polishing that presentation to the board of directors, or at least making a two-minute egg.

But we're not just talking about wasting time.

We're also talking about useless aggravation.

Let's be honest, who really wants to bother with other people? Other people are nothing but trouble. Not only do you have to shower, shave, put on moisturizer, buy clothes, clean up your place, and think up topics of conversation, but the truth is, you never really know who you're dealing with, do you? Even the most low-key, reserved, quiet dinner companion might in fact be an ax murderer, a KGB agent, a demented psychopath, or even a mime.

(What do they always say after these mass murders, anyway? "He always seemed so quiet.") (You'll notice they say the same thing about mimes.)

And even if they're not ax murderers, you know perfectly well that the minute you get involved, they're going to want to go to *their* restaurants and *their* movies and see *their* friends and leave *their* things lying around and sleep with *their* windows open and use *their* toothpaste, or worse, tooth powder, and possibly even want to go to mime shows.

No, no. Far better to remain alone.

And then, of course, we come to rejection. Now, some people suggest that rejection can actually be a good thing. "You're a stronger person for it," they say heartily, perhaps even clapping you on the back. Or, "It's a shared, common human experience." Or even, "Think of it as an opportunity to learn something about yourself."

Let's examine these theories.

ADVANTAGES TO LIVING WITH SOMEONE

Someone to check changes in moles on your back.

ADVANTAGES TO LIVING ALONE

No one to argue with you.
No one to finish off the Oreos.
No one to criticize your driving.
Don't have to hold stomach in.
Can wear sweatsuit whenever feel like it.
Can wash or not wash sweatsuit whenever feel like it.
Don't have to pick sweatsuit up off the floor.
Don't have to use napkins, sweatsuit is fine.
Don't have to use glasses or silverware.
Can call up old flames and hang up when they answer.
Can watch "Mr. Ed" reruns without interference.
Can hurl all the epithets you like at the people on telethons.

It's true, it does take a certain strength to nurse the agonizing pain and bitter, festering bile—especially as each subsequent rejection, piling up into a huge, cumulative, suffocating heap of despair and degradation, eats away at your soul like some grotesque being from Hell.

Too, the "shared experience" aspect cannot be underplayed. Certainly all your friends and co-workers enjoy your pathetic humiliations, snickering behind your back, having parties without inviting you, excluding you from important business functions, perhaps even encouraging the boss to give you the "joke" assignments.

Finally, thinking of it as a "learning opportunity" is not without merit—an opportunity, of course, to recognize that *you're not that cute.* Your fat thighs, your laughable attempts to camouflage your oversized rear end, your short, stumpy little legs (or maybe your tall, geeky long legs), your squinty little rodent eyes, all those little broken capillaries and blotches and spots and scars you never used to have—let's face it, you're pig-ugly, aren't you?

Despite these theories, however, we still think rejection is something to be avoided, if possible. And since sex, as we know, leads almost inevitably to rejection, the question is clear: Why have sex?

The fundamental truth about sex, of course, is that you can always *say* you've had it whether you've had it or not. No one can actually *see* whether you've had it.

Which, of course, brings us to the lynchpin of celibacy and, we might add, in this era of fast-track, fast-paced conspicuous consumption, a key philosophical point of our time:

What's the point of having something no one can see?

TEST YOUR C.Q.
(CELIBACY QUOTIENT)

1. You're invited to a hot party where you won't know many of the people. You:

(a) put on your favorite outfit and look forward to making new friends.

(b) assume the invitation was meant for someone else.

(c) wonder what the hell those pathetic assholes want from you.

2. At the mall, an attractive stranger asks where the elevators are. You:

(a) say, "Why, I was just going there myself."
(b) assume they're talking to someone else and continue on your way.
(c) say, "What, do I look like I work here?"

3. Someone tells you you have nice eyes. You:

(a) thank them graciously and look for something to compliment *them* on in return.
(b) assume they're talking to someone else and leave.
(c) snarl, "If I want your opinion, I'll ask for it."

4. In bed with someone for the first time, you have to get up to go to the bathroom. You:

(a) walk uninhibitedly, self-assuredly into the bathroom.
(b) fall self-consciously to the floor and slither into the bathroom, hoping no one will notice.
(c) shout, "What the fuck are you looking at?" even though your partner is asleep.

5. Your partner suggests a new sexual position. You:

(a) delightedly comply—you're always willing to experiment with possible new horizons of pleasure.
(b) assume they're talking to someone else.
(c) scream, "You filthy pervert!" and throw them out.

6. If there's something particular you'd like your partner to do in bed, you:

(a) suggest it encouragingly, knowing it'll be taken in the spirit of good clean fun.
(b) go to your therapist and whine for three years.
(c) scream, "Don't you know *anything*?"

7. In bed, you make it your business to:

(a) lavish attention on all your partner's erogenous zones.
(b) keep out of trouble.
(c) unplug the chain saw.

8. When exploring your own erogenous zones, you like to use:

(a) scented sensual oils, while relaxing in a warm bath.
(b) surgical gloves.
(c) old issues of *Soldier of Fortune*.

9. During sex, you usually think:

(a) "Sex really brings two people closer together."
(b) "Is that heartburn or you-know-what?"
(c) "Boy, leather really makes me sweat."

10. During sex, you often think it would be better if you were:

(a) on a tropical island.
(b) in a tax audit.
(c) alone.

11. Ideally, you would like to have sex:

(a) 2–3 times a week.
(b) once or twice a year, is that too much to ask?
(c) without your neighbors calling the police.

12. When you can't get sex for a long period of time, you:

(a) sublimate with other pleasurable activities such as sports or nature hikes.
(b) continue in your job as an executive.
(c) have to be subdued by force.

Computing Your Score

Give yourself 10 points for every "a" answer, 5 points for every "b" answer, and 0 points for every "c" answer.

90—120 points: You are friendly, gregarious, meet people easily, have warm, loving relationships, and frequent sex. Don't worry. It *is* possible to change all that.

40—85 points: Fear of intimacy, hypochondria, neurotic insecurity—congratulations! You're well on your way to a sex-free life. But you *do* have those occasional accidental romantic lapses. This book can help you work on those flaws and weak spots.

0—35 points: *Put the book down.* Leave the store quietly. No one is going to hurt you. Thank you.

Part One

HOW NOT TO
MEET PEOPLE

THE TWIN IDEALS:
SLOTH AND SOLITUDE

The purest and most revered strategy for zero sex, of course, is *never leaving your apartment.*

The rise to power of an entire generation dedicated to the idealistic vision of being able to basically just lie around in your room while Mom brings you stuff has spawned a subculture of catalogues and delivery services that bring a song to the heart of any true social misfit. Foods of myriad cuisines, clothing, audio equipment, reverse phone directories, ammunition—all can be made to appear at your door in the twinkling of a touch-tone. The proliferation of TV channels (and the accompanying quality of programming) act as a mind-numbing sedative as you while away your solitary hours.

How could the celibate life be any better? You never need worry about your diet—the fatter the better! And your wardrobe can consist entirely of muu-muus (women) and torn boxer shorts (men) for those occasional unavoidable interactions with delivery boys, landlords, or the FCC.

The only flaw in this Utopian dream, unfortunately, is the difficulty of supporting this enviable lifestyle without having to leave your safe haven.

Sure, you can always become a writer, composer, artist, or telephone swindler. But not everyone has the energy or temperamental strength for the challenge of such a life:

the necessary neurotic compulsiveness ("What kind of paper shall I use? Should I get an electric keyboard or a regular piano? easel or drawing board? touch-tone or pulse dialing?"), the wide mood swings between bleak despair and slightly less bleak despair, and the sheer physical and emotional toll—endless days filled with blank staring, reinvestigating the contents of the refrigerator, and checking to see if the mail has come yet, interspersed with erratic, tiny bursts of marginally productive, pathetic attempts at work.

Most people, then, must venture outside, out into a world fraught with social interactions—business relationships, consumer transactions, accidental encounters, many of them friendly. Can you really succeed in staving off a social life? Of course you can. Don't worry your pretty little head. Just remember, one step at a time. And your first step, naturally, is your choice of job.

JOBS FOR CELIBACY

Ah, the many chances for romance in the workplace. Every day, we read another discouraging article: "Meeting People at Work!" "Love on the Job!" Elevators, hallways, everywhere you turn, apparently, opportunity lurks.

The plum jobs, then, are **jobs with no co-workers at all**—ideally, jobs alone in some tiny enclosure:

Lighthouse keeper
Sentry at the Berlin Wall (East Berlin side)
Beefeater at Buckingham Palace
Tollbooth collector
Forest ranger
Fotomat clerk

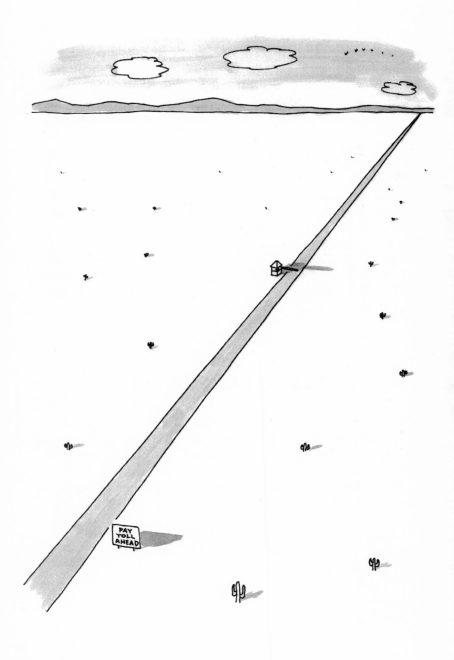

Failing this, your second choice, of course, would be **jobs with minimum human contact**:

Rare books librarian for Zuma Beach City College
Facials salon owner in the Yukon
Sports doctor for MENSA
Sweet 'n Low salesman in Bulgaria
Photo stylist for the Department of Motor Vehicles
Chewing tobacco supplier for the Metropolitan Opera
Tofu chef at Sizzler
Mini-mall developer in the Asian steppes
Real estate agent in Chernobyl
Hayride coordinator for the *New York Review of Books*

These jobs, unfortunately, are usually snapped up the minute they appear. So you may well find yourself obliged to take employment at some sort of firm, with offices, or worse, open cubicles, with watercoolers, elevators, or even, God help us, jolly communal lunchrooms. How, then, can you fend off contact? Again, this can easily be done. Your primary concern should now become your appearance.

CELIBACY MAKEOVER: GETTING THAT REPELLENT "GO YONDER" LOOK

Everyone sometimes has one of those days when you just somehow look fabulously bad. Maybe you've been ill, maybe you're puffy and bloated, or maybe you just happened to throw on a few casual pieces and you look dreadful!

The truth is, you can have that repellent "go yonder" look all the time. Much of it is a matter of *attitude.*

Even if you're feeling thin and somewhat attractive (for you), you can dispel the effect by cultivating a dull, slack-jawed gape. (Be careful not to confuse this with the "moronic stare," which has catapulted many a runway model, rock singer, and vice-presidential candidate to unexpected prominence and undesirable popularity.) In addition, a hostile expression, a bitter frown, or a good, hearty scowl will do wonders for anyone's appearance. Remember what Mother told you: "A smile is the quickest way to make a friend!"

Next, pay attention to the "inner you"—the sour, gaseous you that you so often hide from the rest of the world. Bad general health habits go a long way to achieving that dull, lackluster look.

Here, your motto should be, "Go for it!" Pancakes for breakfast, Snickers for lunch, and a nice big chiliburger for dinner. Eat that extra jelly donut. Cram it in. You can do it! And don't forget the "social helpers"—greasy fried potatoes, carbonated beverages, spicy Mexican food, and, of course, beans.

But the real key to any presentation is, naturally, the packaging. How can *you* get that breezy, easy, "Hey, I'm undesirable!" look?

Surprisingly, it's not that difficult. You need to begin by coordinating your wardrobe around a few key pieces: good, solid classics that immediately bring authority, strength, and that unmistakable "Don't bother" panache to any ensemble.

Women

Gals, if you're going to invest in just one piece, your best bet would be the *garish polyester pants that are too tight in the rear.* These are guaranteed to make any man turn his head, gazing after you with the silent, burning question, "Does she have a license to haul that thing?"

Once you've got this good, solid beginning, you can add to it slowly but surely:

1. That yellowish cardigan from eighth grade that you didn't throw away because it's still useful despite the moth-holes.

2. The blouse where the gap in front is hardly noticeable once you put the safety pin in.

3. The skirt that's too tight but okay once you open the top button and unzip it a little.

4. An extra-large mohair sweater in muddy brown, dirty pink, or dingy pewter.

5. Oversize men's sweatsuits with food stains on them.

6. Swimming gear. Happily, swimsuit designers have spent years designing garments to spotlight our every flaw, so you can pick just about anything in this category, though you may want to start with the "Elephantine" (high-cut maillot), the "Hindenburg" (low-cut maillot), or the "Blubber Parade" (string bikini).

Next, don't forget the wily craft of cosmetics! Here, women have always had a slight edge over men, with those coy little beauty salon tricks and secrets (though men have been rapidly catching up—see below). You might try any of the following looks:

1. The "Aunt Sadie"—lipstick around mouth (don't bother to outline lips; feel free to go anywhere) and on teeth.

2. The "Aunt Rita"—tons of blush in lurid colors; heavy dousing with cheap perfume.

3. "Early Charlie's Angel"—hair teased and sprayed into "wings"; heavily applied, light blue eyeshadow.

4. The "Aunt Yetta"—unplucked eyebrows and moustache.

5. The "kiln owner"—limp, long hair with scraggly split ends and ears sticking out.

Men

As in a women's wardrobe, the well-dressed celibate man's fashion palette revolves around a few key pieces. To begin with, you can never go wrong with a fine, classic pair of *pants with elastic waist (no fly), one size too small.* Slip them on and, instantly, your stomach looks fat, your rear end bulges out, and your legs look like sausages. Best of all, they make any woman wonder exactly *how* you go to the bathroom, and conjure up a vivid image of that pants-around-the-ankle-as-you-stand-at-the-urinal look.

Ideally, these pants should be in a bright primary color or plaid, and are best worn with a slightly small T-shirt, worn riding high, with pants riding low. Black socks complete the turnout.

The more adventuresome might experiment with other possibilities:

1. The "Uncle Max"—roomy, flapping shorts with black socks and garters.

2. Flimsy, too-tight jogging pants (for that "more than you want to see" look).

3. Flared pants and flyaway collars (the "stuck in the last decade" look).

4. Leisure suits.

In terms of "salon options," men have fast been gaining ground in this once exclusively female turf. A good, solid "animal-died-on-my-head" toupee does wonders for any outfit, as does badly but generously applied Man-Tan. And, of course, the various ways you can style your facial hair:

1. The "Las Vegas pimp"—tiny triangle of beard just below lower lip.

2. The "I never got out of the last century"—never-ending sideburns.

3. The "Ultra-repeller"—Fu Man Chu moustache.

One final tip for both men and women: a proper wardrobe is properly cared for. Holes, rips, perspiration stains, split seams—all should be carefully maintained. And make generous use of the many scented products out on the market, such as chemical mothballs (remember, naphthalene repels more than moths!). And don't forget visibly inept self-maintenance—toothpaste drool, burns from the iron, food stains. (See also "Emergency Tips.")

EMERGENCY TIPS

Okay, accidentally you've got on cool jeans, a cool shirt, you look good—and you need to run out for groceries. What can you do? In a pinch, accessorize! Any of these little touches will do the trick:

1. Gray, ratty bra strap showing (or tattered, ancient pair of jockey shorts).
2. Birkenstocks.
3. Unzipped fly.
4. Visible underarm shields.
5. Safety pins, or better yet, electrical tape holding anything together.
6. Flecks of shaving foam and bits of toilet paper.
7. Ski mask (particularly useful if you run out of money and decide to hold up the supermarket).

Well, there you have it. The solid beginnings of a good celibate wardrobe. Now you can turn your attention to the next step: your behavior. Remember, just because you have co-workers doesn't mean they have to talk to you!

DATEPROOFING YOUR WORK ENVIRONMENT

Your first strategy here should be to *make your immediate surroundings as uninviting as possible.* What objects, decor, or interesting accessories might best reflect your goal? Try some of these "starter suggestions":

Any mug, ashtray, or statuette introducing you as a sex
 machine.

Trophies from high school.

Entire desk and surrounding wall covered with pictures
 of your cats.

Bride's magazines (for that "Hello, I want to get married" effect).

Huge picture of Mother.

Half-eaten, rotting liverwurst sandwiches.

Drugstore supplies (see chart below, "10 Things to Buy
 at the Drugstore So Everyone Leaves You Alone").

Roll of toilet paper used as Kleenex.

Then turn your attention to your behavior. During
lunch, around the watercooler, or during important business presentations, loudly make your own contributions:

Eat high-profile food (one good oily fish sandwich can
 get you through an entire day).

Spread rumors.

Ask everyone about your various interesting medical
 symptoms.

Ask male co-workers about penile implants (say loudly,
 "I figured you'd know").

Men: stare at women's breasts and refer to women in
 the plural ("Will you two be going out tonight?").

Pretend to use your handkerchief but actually pick your
 nose.

Goodness gracious, you should have no trouble at all
getting through the day with minimum social contact!
 But what about en route to work? Or over the weekend?
Or legal holidays? Or even those holidays where, okay,

10 THINGS TO BUY AT THE DRUGSTORE
SO EVERYONE LEAVES YOU ALONE

Sure, you can loudly ask the clerk if you rinse out a condom, is it okay to reuse it? But isn't it better, and simpler, just to arm yourself with a couple of highly visible, embarrassing purchases?

1. Enema bag
2. Douches
3. Feminine hygiene spray
4. Masculine hygiene spray
5. Stool softener
6. Ex-Lax
7. Anti-flatulence tablets
8. Bulk pack of Odor-Eaters
9. Jumbo "hospital-size" sanitary napkins
10. Inflatable "donut" pillow

there's no mail, and the banks are closed, but the stores are still open? The possibilities for interaction are neverending.

Again, don't worry. A few simple tips will get you through.

"YOU'RE NOT ONE OF THOSE GUYS WHO'S NEUROTIC ABOUT BEING SO SHORT, ARE YOU?": SUREFIRE NON-PICK-UP LINES

It seems certainly unlikely, if you have mastered the material so far, that anyone might approach *you*. But human nature being what it is, you might occasionally find yourself peculiarly attracted to some stranger and, despite yourself, dangerously interested in beginning a conversation.

This impulse can easily be nipped in the bud. It's simply a matter of using the right approach, or "ice-freezer." Any of these "openers" are surefire!

"Wanna fuck?"

"Hey, the professor said the funniest thing on Gilligan's Island yesterday!"

"Is that a midget flashlight in your pocket, or are you just glad to see me?"

"You're not one of those guys who's neurotic about being so short, are you?"

"I bet you were cute with hair."

"You're not frigid or anything, are you?"

"God, don't you just hate bladder infections?"

"You know, marriage is really important to me."

"You ever consider going on a diet?"

"Well, I guess you'll do. I'm so horny at this point I'd go for anything."

WAYS TO BEHAVE AT A PARTY SO NO ONE WILL COME NEAR YOU

What if you should gain consciousness and happen to find yourself at a party, perhaps filled with lively, amiable people bent on establishing rapport or even conversation? Can you still manage to stave off any sort of human contact?

Of course. The trick is *attitude*. You might try, for example, one of the "popular standards":

"Geek"

Mentally "image" yourself as 13 years old.

Remember, nobody likes you.

Everyone thinks you're dumb.

Everyone's wondering what you're doing here.

Remember the time when your date danced with that other girl for the whole entire eighth grade dance, and even the teachers made fun of you?

Spill red wine.

"Hipper-Than-Thou"

Answer all questions in monosyllables, looking over the person's shoulder.

Wear black.

Respond to everything with snide, dismissive laugh.

If anyone mentions anyplace: "Oh, is that still happening?"

If anyone mentions anyone or anything:

"Oh, is he still in the business?"
"Does anyone still eat there?"
"Oh, I saw it in Cannes."

"The Man Who Would Be Howie"

Talk very loud.
Consider all furniture, knickknacks, hors d'oeuvres,
    and guests' attire grist for your humor mill.
Play any available musical instruments loudly, singing.
Tell host's parents really dirty jokes.
Insist on organizing manic party activities involving
    water balloons, phony phone calls, and harassing the
    pizza delivery boy.
Pull out tablecloths (don't worry, no need to practice).

Part Two

DATING DON'TS
AND DON'TS

DATE PREVENTION:
IN THE EVENT OF A PHONE CALL

Unlikely as it may seem, every so often someone may call you up. They may be judgment-impaired or temporarily delusional, or perhaps you come from a culture where such things are arranged by people inimical to your interests, such as your family.

Worse, these calls frequently come without previous warning, catching you completely off guard. There you are, slumped on the sofa in your muu-muu, watching the nightly news, when there is a strange, jarring, unfamiliar sound—the ringing of the phone. To your horror, it's that darkly handsome man from work, inexorably bent on extending some sort of invitation.

But there's no need to panic. He could be calling for any number of reasons! Quickly, examine the most likely possibilities:

1. He thinks you're somebody else.
2. He dialed your number by accident and now he's too embarrassed to admit it.
3. He's forgotten what you look like.
4. His friends put him up to this as a joke (in fact, isn't that them you hear giggling in the background?).
5. It's part of a sadistic fraternity hazing ritual.
6. He just wants something from you.

7. Not even sex! He just wants to manipulate you into putting in a good word with the boss!

8. No! Not even that! He doesn't think anyone cares what you'd say! No, he probably wants you to *type* something for him!

Now, no matter what he says, you can snarl, "What's the matter, your arm broke?" Then you can go back to your tuna melt and Tom Brokaw. (Of course, if Tom Brokaw calls, you may want to alter this method somewhat. For example: "What's the matter, *Mr. Anchorman*, your arm broke?")

In a far more disturbing vein, however, sometimes, hideously, we are actually compelled, despite our better judgment, to call someone ourselves and ask them out. Yes, this does happen.

Often, this urge can be dealt with by a brief, honest examination of one's personal attributes. But occasionally, in a wretched, besotted burst of false optimism, and despite a clear sense-memory of your last misbegotten encounter with another human being, you find yourself pathetically, uncontrollably reaching for the phone.

DON'T PANIC. There's still plenty of time for a firm de-pep talk (or "dyspepsia"). Sure, she's been smiling encouragingly at you for the past six weeks, but so what? You've got imagination! Use it!

1. What if she's not sure who you are?

2. What if she says no?

3. What if she thinks you'd be really boring?

4. What if she thinks you'd take her someplace lousy?

5. What if she thinks you'd take her someplace classy, but everyone would see her with you and she'd be embarrassed?

6. What if she thinks you'd have a really dumb car?

7. What if she thinks you wouldn't be that good a driver?

8. What if she thinks you wouldn't be that good in bed?

9. Hey, where does she get off making judgments?

10. Who says *she's* so hot?

11. Who died and made *her* queen?

Now you are in a prime state of mind to call her up and scream, "Hey, I didn't want to go out with you anyway!" This should ensure a string of dateless Saturdays for you.

SARAJEVO: A DATE ERUPTS

But sometimes, alas, in one of those fickle, aberrant twists of fate, a rendezvous, a tête-à-tête, a date is achieved. Yes, you have failed to be unpleasant enough, or accidentally agreed to some sort of meeting—perhaps, gruesomely, on a Friday or Saturday night.

There's no use understating this. It's very, very serious. *Dates can often lead to sex.* But with effort—and a little luck—it's still certainly possible to prevent this from happening.

The first thing to remember is to *think positively.* You *can* win this battle. You *can* win this war. You have destroyed evenings before and you will destroy evenings again. Some you will destroy abruptly and cleanly, like the swift fall of a well-aimed executioner's ax; others will die a slow and lingering death.

The point is to have an evening with you remembered as a truly unique experience, somewhat like leprosy or a really bad car accident. You want to *prevent this person from ever going out with you again.*

This may seem difficult at first. After all, your date has already shown a psychotic inability to distinguish right from wrong in making the date to begin with. However, there are a number of skills you can learn and exercise. Like a good golf swing, or operating a guillotine, these skills become easier and more natural the more you use them, and soon you'll be doing them without even thinking!

THE DREADED DINNER DATE

Many a plan for zero sex has been sadly derailed by a quiet, candlelit dinner à deux in some romantic little bistro, trattoria, or even Rathaus. And so what should you do if some sort of evening meal has, somehow, irrevocably been engendered?

Over the years, innumerable methods for ruining dinners have been tested and refined (first of all, in your choice of partners you might wish to consult our earlier book, *Getting That "Eva Braun" Luck Every Time*). But even with the most dangerously attractive or interesting companion, it's absolutely possible to emerge successfully sexless from the fray.

Your first and key weapon, of course, should be *your conversational skills*. As you and your date study the menus, for example, you might try any of the following openers:

"That's a really slimming outfit."
"Are you sure you want to order something that fattening?"
"You know, a good dermatologist could fix that."
"Did you fart?"

16 ACTIVITIES TO SUGGEST IF
YOU GAIN CONTROL OVER THE DATE

Getting your car oiled and lubed (remember to snicker suggestively at the word "lubricate").

Doing your laundry.

Taking your dog to be put to sleep.

Going to your therapist ("This is the one I've been telling you about").

Going to your accountant to do your taxes.

Going to the gynecologist (especially effective if you are a man).

Doing your paper route (usually used by the younger crowd, but can be usefully offputting in a thirty-five-year-old man).

Renewing your driver's license.

Filing for unemployment.

Making a drug drop-off.

Defrosting your refrigerator.

Shampooing your rugs.

Shopping for clothes for another, more important date.

Shopping for a new couch.

Bingeing.

Any activity involving your relatives.

Then, you might segue to any of the myriad tried-and-true topics:

Yourself
Your childhood
Your early years
Your relationship with your mother
Your relationship with your father

Your health

How horrible all your previous relationships were and
   how it was always their fault

Your favorite jokes from last night's "Tonight Show"
   monologue

Your decision on who Johnny's successor will be

Your analysis of the Johnny/Ed relationship

How hard it is to find someone who understands you

Social skills, of course, should also be brought into play.
For women, if the man's paying, it's always a nice touch to
order the most expensive item on the menu. And dig in
heartily! "Lawsy me, I sure do love a nice slab of beef!" you
might bellow, or simply, "Moo!"

Today's new "food awareness" has brought an entirely
new arsenal of culinary weaponry into the dating trenches.
The so-called "breath foods"—for example, onions, garlic,
and Gorgonzola cheese—are good starters, and don't rule
out the lesser-known nose-turners: sardines, which pro-
vide the highly amusing "cat breath," or curry, which
seeps out of the pores for at least twenty-four hours.

Foods high in awkwardness quotient, or the "geek foods,"
are also useful. Lobster provides not only the "soaking
your date for all he's worth" angle but also the opportunity
to wear a bib and smear your chin with butter—not to be
underrated! Corn on the cob, asparagus, and artichokes
are also not to be shortchanged, and don't forget our old
friend, unboned fish! Not only do you spend the entire
dinner picking little spiny things, and perhaps entire
blobs of chewed-up debris, out of your mouth, but at any
moment you might choke! There's nothing like a good
Heimlich maneuver to dampen even the most ardent
suitor, especially if it's unsuccessful.

And, in a pinch, you can always turn to the old standby,

getting food caught between your teeth. Few things en-
hance a moronic grin more than a good old-fashioned
poppy seed. Bits of your charbroiled steak, remnants of
your spinach salad, and even strawberry seeds are also
fine candidates. (Don't be afraid to sit there, picking food
out of your teeth with your fingers, or better yet, bring
dental floss to the table!)

And don't rule out nouvelle cuisine! Crème brulée can
often lead to ten or even fifteen minutes of working away
at sticky caramel embedded in your bicuspids. Now,
surely, your date will beg to be taken home, as soon as
possible, and what more could you ask for?

ENJOYING YOURSELF
AND HOW TO THWART IT

But what if you find yourself veering toward enjoying
yourself? Perhaps your date has the bluest eyes you've
ever seen, or the sweetest smile, or a delicate musical
laugh like distant cowbells in a verdant Alpine meadow.
Here, perhaps, a quick mental exercise is the most useful
way to stop these fruitless thoughts. As you're ordering
dinner, simply *imagine the rest of the date*:

You're going to be charming, you're going to tell her
your funniest stories, even that surefire one about that
time you got locked out of your apartment, you'll spend a
fortune on the dinner; you'll take her to the latest movie,
you'll tell her all your best stories about the stars and the
real dirt on the making of the movies and how they really
did those stunts, then you'll bring her back to your place,
which you've even cleaned for the occasion, and then the

second you *touch* her, for Christ's sake, she'll launch into this whole speech about how she just got out of a relationship, she needs some time to get her head together, she thinks you're really funny and sweet but she's not looking to get involved with anyone for a while, let's just be friends, well fuck her!

Now, even before the appetizer arrives, you should be back to your customary level of oafish surliness.

But supposing you still find yourself leaning dangerously toward her, your knees touching ever so casually under the table, her jasmine-scented perfume gently wafting closer? As the appetizer arrives, *imagine the whole relationship*:

You'll go out, you'll agree on everything, you'll like all the same movies, food, places, sex has never been better, you make each other laugh, you buy each other cute presents, maybe those little koalas that attach to your rearview mirror, or little teddy bears with cute T-shirts, you get along with each other's friends, you spend every night together and decide why not move in, you're living together so why not get married, you have a simple but moving ceremony outdoors as the sun is setting, now you're married, you have a baby, then the twins come, you get a bigger house, she gets a promotion, now she's working directly with Steve, the senior vice-president, there are all these messages from Steve every day, she starts working later and later, suddenly the business trips start, you have to pretend you don't notice anything, meanwhile you're left driving the twins to the scout meetings, not to mention Adam's soccer practice three times a week, then one day she comes home and announces she can't go on with this charade, it's nothing personal, she's grown one way and you've grown another, she's moving in with Steve, you're stuck with the kids, she doesn't want to hurt you and hopes you can still be friends, well fuck her!

Again, this should make short shrift of the jasmine, not to mention that grating, bovine cackle.

Women, of course, may find themselves equally swayed: a crinkly grin, a manly forearm, a certain tough yet vulnerable bravado—danger signs all! Again, the same techniques are recommended:

He's going to figure because he spent money on me, he gets to sleep with me. He thinks I'm worth the price of a piece of chicken and a Diet Coke. And this isn't even free-range chicken. They probably don't even have espresso here. I don't *see* an espresso machine. Wait, is that the sound of high-pressure steam? [Please try not to get distracted during these exercises.]

He's going to treat me shabbily. If I sleep with him tonight, he'll think I'm easy. He'll come too quickly, then he'll be embarrassed and blame me, then he'll fall asleep and snore loudly and take all the blankets and thrash around and crowd me out of bed and look surprised to see me in the morning.

Who needs this kind of humiliation? Not to mention having to listen to that endless idiotic story about him being locked out of his apartment. Go to the ladies' room and sneak out and take a cab home. Heat up a Lean Cuisine, hop into bed, and watch the late news (or the early news, depending on how soon you've come to your senses). With repetition, the likelihood of the situation arising will decrease sharply!

BEYOND DINNER:
WHEN FUN THREATENS

But what if it's not dinner à deux, you may ask? What if your date has dreadfully planned some thoughtful, entertaining activity that the two of you might actually enjoy?

Don't be such a goofy gus. You can bring your surly unpleasant personality into *any* situation! Often it's just as simple as knowing the right questions to ask! Remember, you want the memory of your evening together to linger on, like the stench of some poisonous gas.

At a Football Game

"Why do they play with a pointy ball?"
"Wait, weren't they just going the other way?"
"Is he dead?"
"Wouldn't that hurt?"
"Do you think any of them are dating the cheerleaders?"
"What's the big deal? It's only a *game.*"

At a Broadway Play

Yelling:

"Oh, I bet I know what's gonna happen!"
"What? What? I didn't hear what he said!"
"Who's that? Where'd she come from?"
"I wonder how long this is going to be. I'm hungry."

Singing along loudly (whether or not it is a musical).
Mooning the actors.

Participating in Recreational Sports

(Basically, the key here is *strategic whining.*)

"I hurt my leg."
"I hurt my arm."
"I hurt my finger."
"I chapped my lips."
"I think I'm getting a new freckle."

At the Movies

Female nude scene (male reaction)

"What a big butt she has!"
"God, I hate women all out of proportion like that."
"Boy, she looks a lot fatter naked."

Male nude scene (female reaction)

Pointing and going, "Oh, no!"
Hysterical laughter.
"Look at that little thing!"
"Where is it?"
"Boy, what a letdown!"

Any kind of exposure of skin

(Loudly) "Well, *hello* there!"

GENERALLY USEFUL BEHAVIOR
DURING ANY PART OF THE DATE

Walking down dark alleyways, shouting threats at people in
    shadowy doorways.
Imitating Robert de Niro in *Taxi Driver.*
Imitating Robert de Niro in *The Godfather.*
Imitating Robert de Niro in *Bang the Drum Slowly.*
Tailgating and yelling at other drivers.
If stopped by cops, making sudden movement toward glove
    compartment (just to crack them up).
Driving in expensive car through poverty-stricken parts of town
    and shouting inflammatory comments out of window.
Vomiting.

READING THE SIGNS: HOW TO
MAKE SHALLOW SNAP JUDGMENTS

What if, through some dreadful series of mishaps, and
despite all your efforts to the contrary, you find yourself
increasingly, disastrously attracted to your date?

Don't worry. Like any escalating skirmish, it can still be
stopped.

The secret here is a little more sophisticated—but, once
you learn it, amazingly simple. The trick is *learning how
to interpret the hidden signs,* those tiny giveaway ges-
tures that can tell you so much about a person, especially
if your goal is to avoid at all costs any sort of emotional
involvement.

Learning to "read" body language gives you an invaluable shorthand, a swift and ready tool to instantly abrogate any dangerously budding interest. Yes, it *is* absolutely possible to remain on a completely safe, shallow level of noninvolvement. All you need to do is to train yourself to recognize—and decode—the key "signs."

Woman won't unlock car door for man	Doesn't engage in oral sex
Man gets in car without opening door for woman	No foreplay
Can't hail a cab	Impotent
Insists on going to a brand-new restaurant	Prefers virgins
Insists on going to a brand-new restaurant but gets lost on the way	Is a virgin
Insists on going to romantic, candlelit restaurant	Compulsive Don Juan
Insists on going to homey little cafe with windmill motif	Compulsive Don Quixote
Insists on going to Polynesian bar	Compulsive Don Ho
Wants to go to a French restaurant	Will swallow
Wants to go to a deli	Won't swallow
Uses Sweet 'n Low	Wearing falsies

Takes too long deciding what to order	Has trouble reaching orgasm
Orders salad dressing on the side	Will give you hand job but will not go "all the way"
Gives explicit orders to waiter	Will expect incredibly skillful gymnastics in bed
Asks for extra rolls	Will say she's using birth control when she's not, will get pregnant, and sue you for paternity
Insists on ordering for you, referring to you as "The lady will have . . ."	Thinks you had an orgasm when you didn't
Asks for "the usual"	Insists on missionary position only
Asks what the specials are	Will want you to use handcuffs
Fills up on bread and crackers	Premature ejaculator
Doesn't finish everything on plate	Has already come
Insists on eating some of whatever you ordered	Will make you sleep on wet spot
Changes mind after ordering	Will never call you
Changes table	Nymphomaniac
Drinks decaf	Fakes orgasms (female)

Orders in French	Fakes orgasms (male)
Sends food back	Will sleep with you, brag to all his friends, then try to borrow money
Asks for detailed description of desserts	Needs you to talk dirty during sex
Orders a dessert involving ladyfingers	Wants hand job
Orders a dessert involving nuts	Castrating bitch
Wants to split dessert	Is dying to get rid of her apartment, move in with you, rearrange all your closets, and take down all your baseball posters
Credit card is refused	Low sperm count
Undertips waiter	Small penis
Undertips parking valet	Small penis
Undertips cabbie	Small penis
Uses toothpick	Is trying to tell you size isn't everything
Removable cassette player in car	Pulls out repeatedly during sex
Cellular phone in car	Penile implant

AFTER-DINNER DRINKS—
WHAT THEY SHOW ABOUT A MAN

Port—will fall asleep immediately after sex.
Brandy—will leave immediately after sex.
Drambuie—will fall asleep during sex.
Cognac—will leave during sex.

GENERAL MENU CHOICES—
WHAT THEY REVEAL IN A WOMAN

Orders steak—is looking for sex.
Orders chicken—is looking for a relationship.
Orders salad—has picked out wedding dress, bridesmaids,
and caterer.

Part Three

POST-DATE PITFALLS
AND HOW TO FIND THEM

THE REPELLENT APARTMENT: DECORATING TIPS

Always remember what Mother used to tell you—you never know when you'll have an unexpected guest. (Certainly the statistical probabilities, given your personality, are slight, but perhaps Mother was speaking in the broadest mathematical terms. Perhaps Mother was a statistician. Did you ever think of that? No. That's your problem. You just don't think, do you?)

For example, what if, despite all your well-practiced efforts to the contrary, you inexplicably find your date coming home with you? You've tried everything, including swerving the car suddenly, hoping they'll fall out, but they're still there! How could this have happened?

Well, it's no use getting into a philosophical discussion now. The important thing to realize is, yes, this can happen, even to you, and you need to be prepared. Many a date has gotten all the way to the front door, even inside an apartment, only to be swiftly repulsed by a properly mobilized decor.

You might want to begin with "basic disarray" (proceeding from there to "advanced disarray," "hurricane," and "I think someone may have broken in and ransacked the place, but I'm not sure"): piles of dirty laundry strewn around, every dish you own out on the counter (unwashed), strangely textured objects in your refrigerator, a shower curtain that has taken on a life of its own—oh, and isn't that the cat litter box over there? Your date may not even stay around to see your beer can collection!

But what if they do? What if they sit down on the couch, make themselves comfortable, and plainly seem inclined to make themselves at home?

Perhaps you might want your apartment to reveal a little bit more about yourself. A deeper, even more unappetizing (if that could be possible) self:

HOW TO MAKE YOUR APARTMENT REVEAL UNAPPEALING PERSONALITY TRAITS IN YOU

You can tell an immense amount about someone by seeing how they decorate their home. Are they adventuresome? conservative? ax murderers? grifters? Even a brief visit can be revealing (pay special attention to little details like whetstones and honing devices).

With just a little effort, you too can learn to present yourself through your furnishings. Consider, perhaps, some of these popular styles:

Women

The "Venus Flytrap"

Thirsty, man-size terrycloth robe in bathroom.
Complete collection of any liquor a man could want.
Naughty lingerie strewn around the bed.
Bride's magazines strewn around.

Brochures for the Poconos, Niagara Falls, the Caribbean.

Books in bookcase: *How to Meet a Man, How to Dress to Attract a Man, How to Make a Man Fall in Love with You, How to Make a Man Marry You, How to Make a Man Buy You a Mink Coat, a House on Long Island, Lots of Jewelry, and a Mercedes-Benz.*

"Fat Girl Waiting to Happen"

Same as above, only with frozen cheesecake in the freezer.

"Mom"

Darning basket and sewing machine open and ready to darn date's sweater ("So, we'll miss the beginning of the movie, is that the end of the world?").

Knitting (something to do at the movies).

Overstocked pantry and refrigerator ("Eat it, it'll only go bad").

Home Medical Encyclopedia (for alerting waiter to date's allergies at dinner).

"Daddy's Little Girl"

Quilt with cute bears on it.

Tea set with cute bears on it.

Dinner plates with cute bears on them.

Rugs, lamps, linens, clothing, and crocheted toilet-paper covers with cute bears on them.

Fuzzy stuffed animals arranged all over the bed.

Doorstop in shape of dachshund (cute bear not available).

Picture of self and Daddy.

"Ms. Intimidation"

Snarling dog.

Odd pieces of equipment that might be for mountain-climbing but you're not sure.

Video camera, with professional lights and umbrellas, next to bed.

Men

"The Prince"

Picture of self working out with Dodgers.

Picture of self doing business with Donald Trump.

Picture of self cooking with Paul Bocuse.

Picture of self with famous plumber in bathroom.

Home movies of self transferred to video (VHS, Beta, and PAL/SECAM).

Bookcase including titles such as: *Women Who Love Too Much and Where to Find Them* and *Premature Ejaculation—That's Her Problem.*

Map of world with little pushpins showing where he's been.

Computer with specially designed program coordinating his outfits.

"Mommy's Little Boy"

Refrigerator full of containers from home.

Cupboards full of nice, nourishing breakfast foods.

Telephone with first four speed-dialing slots all various places to reach Mommy.

Many birthday cards hanging up.

Big bags of laundry to take home.
Nametags in clothes and underwear.

"What Overcompensation?"

6-foot-tall stereo speakers.
4-poster bed with over-sized bedposts.
Extremely tall plants.
Industrial-size flashlights (used by policemen and as-
tronauts, you know, I'm not kidding).
Large peppermill.
Extralong TV remote-control device.
Hand mirror with one very specific portion a magnify-
ing mirror.

"Couch Potato Waiting to Happen"

Next week's *TV Guide*, dog-eared, shows circled in red.
Telltale lumpen indentation in couch.
Small refrigerator next to couch.
Mini-microwave to heat up nachos.
House full of useless kitchen gadgets and peculiar
record collections not available in any store.
Lapses into depression when Johnny's in Wimbledon.

GETTING TO "NO":
USEFUL WAYS TO ASK FOR SEX

But supposing a brief tour of your living quarters fails to
do its usual job?

Suppose the hours have drifted by, and you and your
date are sitting on the couch, slowly drifting closer to-

gether, smiling, laughing, sharing a private thought or two. . . .

Surely, you ask, in moments like these, there must be some surefire phrases, carefully worded bons mots guaranteed to lead to celibacy?

Well, of course, there are no guarantees in life, especially not for people who use phrases like "bons mots," but—as your date leans closer and looks meltingly into your eyes—why not try whispering smoothly:

"You gonna let me into your pants, or what?"
Or perhaps:
"Wanna play hide the salami?"
"Y'know, I could really use some action."
"Wanna meet the wangbone?"
And don't forget, in an emergency, the officious:
"Here, babe, let me teach you a few things."

Women, likewise, might try gazing doelike into their date's eyes and murmuring:

"Bet you can't make me come!"
Or:
"My husband used to do it for two hours—think you can break his record?"
(Snapping fingers impatiently): "C'mon, let's see it."
(Sighing): "I guess you won't shut up till we do."
And there's always the succinct:
"This better be good."

You might also try asking your companion coyly if he would care to visit "love's pavilion," "the house under the hill," or simply, "the place where Uncle Doodle goes."

"NO": PERMANENTLY EFFECTIVE WAYS TO REFUSE IT

But what, you may ask, happens in the bizarre eventuality that your date asks *you*? Perhaps in a gentle, romantic way? Ardent, yet hesitant? Sweet, yet taut with barely controlled desire? (My, aren't *we* popular!)

Just try any of these useful responses:

"No."
"Not if my life depended on it."
"I'd rather take the SATs over."
"You're kidding, right?"
"As if you could."
"*Me* and *you*? Come *on*."
Hysterical laughter and "Wait till I tell everybody about this!"
"What are you, nuts?"
"Don't make me throw up."
"I just don't think I could bring myself to."
"Can't you see I'm busy?"
"I'm sorry, I have really high standards."
"Please, I just ate."
"Not if the survival of the human race depended on it."

See? You really shouldn't have any problems.

BEYOND THE HEADACHE: "HAVE YOU READ *THE SUN ALSO RISES*?"— NEW, IMPROVED EXCUSES

For the subtler-minded, let's not forget the old standby, the Medical Excuse. For years, the headache has been the Grande Dame of celibacy. But why shackle yourself with a cliché when there are so many more interesting, unusual excuses to proffer?

Lumbago
Catarrh
Chilblains
Blains
Narcosis of the deep
Hypoglycemia
The bends
Tennis elbow
TMJ
Shin splints
Beriberi
Torn rotator cuff
Seasonal affective disorder

LINGERIE FOR CELIBACY (THAT ELUSIVE AUNT YETTA/ UNCLE MAX LOOK)

But now let's suppose the beriberi failed to work its usual magic. And your sour ripostes have served not a whit to dampen your date's ardor.

GOOD REACTIONS TO SEEING SOMEONE NAKED FOR THE FIRST TIME

Barely masking a look of disappointment.
Stifled laughter.
Confusion.
Terrified scream.
Yawn.
Saying, "Oh no, forget it."
Taking out a magnifying glass.
Suddenly remembering a previous appointment.

Even worse, matters seem to have taken an ugly turn. Your date is undressing you! Her delicate, feminine fingers are fumbling with your manly buttons, your manly belt, and perhaps even your manly zipper (or maybe your strong, masculine hands are making short shrift of her frills, her furbelows, and even the safety pins in her waistband).

At moments like this, you certainly want to be dressed for the occasion.

The classic "lingerie for celibacy" look is not that hard to achieve:

The "Uncle Max"

Torn, flapping boxer shorts, accompanied by pensive scratching.

Black socks with garters.

The "Aunt Yetta"

Enormous, loose, cotton waist-high underpants.

Large white industrial-strength bra, if possible with full corset attachment.

Beige stockings rolled down to just above the knee.

The more adventuresome may want to elaborate: Underwear with days of the week, or better yet, months on them.

Frayed thermal underwear.

Men's bikinis with "Home of the Whopper" or "Slippery When Wet" slogans.

That special, twenty-year-old ratty bathrobe.

But don't forget, if these fortifications fail, there's always attitude!

Part Four

INADVERTENTLY HAVING SEX: EMERGENCY MEASURES

Oh my God, you're naked in bed with somebody! How did this happen? What, are they blind or something?

All right, all right. Calm down. Even if he's sensuously caressing your curvaceous, voluptuous (all right, fat, piglike) body or you're languorously succumbing to his taut, straining (all right, soft, doughy) embrace, try not to panic. First of all, as you well know, it's extremely unlikely to happen again. Secondly, there are a number of steps you can take to minimize the damage—techniques and skills you can use to learn how to have sex without pleasure (for you *and* your partner). Eventually you can master the art of bringing the whole futile mess to a grinding, unpleasant halt!

EXPLORING THE NON-EROGENOUS ZONES (THE "E" SPOT, THE "H" SPOT, THE "HORSE LATITUDES," AND OTHERS)

Bad sex, first of all, involves your entire body—what we might call your "non-erogenous zones." Researchers have identified a number of these areas:

The "E" spot: Your elbow—smashing it against the head-board or, perhaps, a cement wall, leaving it tingling painfully or perhaps even partially paralyzed for the rest of the sorry encounter.

The "H" spot: Your hair—getting it caught in the headboard, under your partner's arm, in the car seat, or in the hinges of your protective goggles.

The "F" spot: Icy feet (yours or your partner's).

The "N" spot: Icy nose (your inquisitive dog's).

The "horse latitudes": Acquiring a painful Charley horse in your leg.

The "A" spot: Partner on top, mashes head painfully into your carotid artery, cutting off blood supply to your brain.

The "L" spot: An alternate to the above; partner squashes all air out of your lungs.

The "B" spot: Female accidentally knees partner in unusually sensitive masculine spot.

And, to try on vacation:

The "S" spot: Exploring areas with sunburn.

PLEASURE PREVENTION: LEARNING TO SELF-DISTRACT (SPECIAL TECHNIQUES TO TRY WITH YOUR PARTNER)

Bad sex, of course, is not just a matter of technique. It's also the spirit and passion you bring to it. Often it's just a matter of simply being yourself (and Lord knows how well that usually serves you). But sometimes it may help to follow certain suggestions or ideas.

You may have already secretly thought of many of these things, or suspected that your friends, judging by their social lives, are already doing them. Certainly we can assure you that, whether they admit to it or not, many people have tried these methods and found them effective. And no matter how experienced you are, you may simply enjoy the variety!

For the woman:

Just lying there like a lox.
Lying there stiffly, tensing every muscle that gets touched.
Asking, "Are we still doing it?"

For the man:

Whistling during foreplay.
Asking, "How long has this been going on?"
Singing, "I'd wait a million years."
Complaining endlessly about how long the woman takes.
Asking, "Got any sisters?"

Things to do during sex (man or woman):

Taking phone calls.
Returning phone calls.
Calling office for messages.
Using remote control to switch TV channels.
Picking off peeling wallpaper.
Reshellacking the headboard.

Rewiring the lamp.

Watching a game show.

Answering questions on game show.

Calling in to volunteer to be on game show.

If a refrigerator is handy, making a sandwich.

Better yet, a milkshake ("Could you go a little faster?").

Flossing your teeth.

Doing your tax returns.

But wait a minute. Who said bad sex only has to be in bed? Why not try more exotic locales? Perhaps an unusual setting might inspire you to even greater heights of imaginative behavior:

In the car: Is this a good time to reorganize the glove compartment?

Outdoors: plant some bulbs?

Bathroom of airplane: stock up on little soaps.

The beach: add to your seashell collection.

In the host's bedroom, upstairs during a party: reorganize host's sock drawer.

In a motel: oh good, more little soaps.

In an office:

Yours: answer mail.

Theirs: make free long-distance phone calls.

A stranger's: see what projects their company has going on.

In a park: weed crabgrass.

In a shower/bath: recaulk tile grout.

AVOIDING ORGASM: YES, YOU CAN!

Disaster! Panic! You are actually about to enjoy yourself sexually! Red alert! Mayday! Mayday!

How on earth did this happen?

There's no time to think of that now. Quickly, move into Emergency Mode: *Thought Control.*

Many men and women have found that the correct train of thought can successfully ruin even the most erotic sexual encounter. Remember, your brain is your most complicated (and in many cases, your biggest) sexual organ.

All it takes is a little practice—learning to focus and concentrate your thoughts. As your breath comes harder and your skin begins to flush, a delicate sheen of sweat coating your thrusting bodies, try to think, perhaps, about arms control. Are we giving away too many nuclear weapons? Are the Russians' tracking capabilities in fact inferior? And, frankly, how can we ever be certain that our monitoring methods are accurate? On the other hand, are we spending too much on weapons when hunger is still a worldwide problem? Speaking of hunger, I could have something to eat.

See? Easy as pie. Or you might want to try domestic issues: are you missing "Saturday Night Live"? Or is it not on this week? Wait a minute, there's that wrestling special, I think. . . .

Once you get more experienced, you can range through a panoply of possibilities. Just remember, as you feel yourself about to enjoy yourself, train your mind to jump into gear—moving into one of those little reveries you know so well (and speaking of pie, a piece of lemon meringue could go down pretty good right about now, couldn't it?):

Women

1. I'm so fat. I'm like a pig. I'm probably flattened out all over the bed. He's probably totally disgusted. I wonder if there's any position I could get into where I wouldn't look totally bovine. Why did I eat so much at dinner? Did I need that chocolate mousse pie? No, of course not. I wonder if he noticed. Why do I always eat so much? Why can't I ever think of anything other than food?

2. God, did I remember to go grocery shopping? I bet there isn't any food in the house. I've got to get more organized. Starting tomorrow, I'll make lists for everything. Groceries, errands, I could have an "A" list for top priorities and a "B" list for ongoing things, like furniture . . .

3. I wonder if I should redecorate? Let's see, I could put some shelves over by the window, then maybe I could have a flower pot or two, maybe a few books, even display my penguin collection . . .

4. He's going to hurt me. He's never going to call. He thinks I'm easy, he thinks I do this with everyone, he's probably comparing me to his ex-girlfriend. He's probably planning to get back with his ex-girlfriend right now. I bet she's really thin.

5. I'm never going to come.

Men

1. She seems so distracted.

2. I wonder if the light's hitting the top of my head?

3. I wonder if there's any food in the house. Probably not, the way she was hogging that chocolate mousse pie at dinner.

4. She's gong to hurt me. She's probably just using me to get back at some ex-boyfriend, probably some really good-looking, simpleminded jerk with a great car. A BMW, or a Mercedes, or maybe even a Ferrari. How do these guys afford those cars, that's what I want to know!

5. I really should get a better job. A guy my age, I should be pulling down more dough. I'm not so young anymore. Kind of getting along, to tell you the truth.

6. What if I had a heart attack right now?

7. What if I had a heart attack, and then she had one of those vaginal spasms, like in *Hollywood Wives*, and I got trapped, and we had to be taken to the hospital? I bet that could really happen! Even worse, what if I tried to write about it and my writing came out like Jackie Collins?

8. She's never going to come.

Certainly, by now you should be well out of the whole mess and watching the hockey game (or perhaps having some lemon meringue pie).

But what if somehow your valiant efforts have failed? What if you've accidentally completed the act, perhaps even enjoying it?

FENDING OFF AFTERGLOW

All right, it's two minutes later. You've had sex.

Don't lie there basking like an idiot. (And wipe that smirk off your face, Mister). Just because you've failed in celibacy doesn't mean there aren't still many fine opportunities for destroying intimacy (and ensuring celibacy for a long, long time into the future).

For many people, the moments directly after sex are even more important than the act itself.

Your best course of action is to leap up quickly, push your partner out of the way, race to the shower, turn the shower on full blast—hot, using industrial-strength soap and disinfectant (and, if possible, loofahs) to rid yourself of every last trace of your partner's musk—then jump into your car and drive off.

But what if they came over to your place? Oh, for heaven's sake, how *do* you get yourself into these fixes?

Well, you might try shoving your partner out of bed, changing the sheets, and spraying the room with pesticides. Certainly any attempts on your partner's part to whisper affectionate little endearments into your ear should be swiftly rebuffed with snarled rejoinders such as "What's it to you?", "As if I care," or "Hey, could you keep it down, I'm trying to watch the game."

Likewise, attempts to touch you anywhere on your body should be met with, "Are you through?" "Get *off* me," "Hey, this is *my* side of the bed," or merely a high-pitched scream.

But sometimes none of these methods work. Five, ten minutes have passed and you're still in bed together. You may even have already tried to call all your buddies up to come over and watch the tape of last night's hockey game and they're not even home!

You've even tried any or all of the traditional last-minute excuses:

LAST-MINUTE EXCUSES
TO NOT SPEND THE NIGHT

Must tend to livestock (dogs, cats, turtles, ant farm).
Allergic to their pillows.
New issue of *Newsweek* arrived that day and haven't read it yet.
Must finish food spoiling in your refrigerator.
Have ordered pizza and want to beat Domino delivery guy to your home.
Must drop off overdue videotapes.
Have to get up early for farm shows in morning.
Trying out new refrigerator deodorizer and want to see if it works.
Cannot use unwaxed dental floss.
May have already won $10,000,000 in Publisher's Clearinghouse Sweepstakes.

Worse, a terrible drowsiness is coming over you, an inexorable, languorous stupor. You can't fight it anymore. You're going to spend the night!

SPENDING THE NIGHT:
YOUR WORST BEHAVIOR YET!

Few things can be as memorable as the first night you spend with someone new. Hopefully, it will also be the last night, so you doubly want it to be an unforgettable experience.

And who could forget the sight of you sprawled gracelessly across the bed like a beached whale, eyes closed, head back, mouth open, drooling slightly, mumbling in your sleep as you hog the blankets in your viselike grip.

You might train yourself to thrash and fling about in the bed, kicking your partner, talking, shouting, breathing your garlic breath all over everything, snorting and wheezing, possibly singing old camp songs and show tunes as you toss and turn into the night.

Another alternative is to make your partner stay up all night as you tell them your life story (all the really good parts you left out during the date).

And don't forget that special intimacy of seeing one another the following morning, rumpled and dewy-eyed, as you awaken and stare balefully at each other. Perhaps some unusual allergy will have caused your eyes to swell shut in the night!

Now is a good time to force your partner into a brisk set of military-style calisthenics, followed by a bracing cold shower (for yourself—they, meanwhile, would be busy cooking you the large farm-style breakfast you have demanded).

Who could ever forget a night with you?

And, certainly, who would ever want to repeat it?

Part Five

IT'S NEVER TOO LATE: CELIBACY AFTER MARRIAGE

Celibacy is fun for young people, but what about people in long-range monogamous relationships, or even married couples?

Don't worry! Marriage is an excellent place to practice celibacy, as many an executive (female or male) will assure you.

FACE CREAM AND BOXER SHORTS: THE MARITAL BOUDOIR

For years, thousands of men and women in colder climates have known the secret of the traditional celibate boudoir attire: T-shirt, sweatshirt, jogging pants, and hiking socks. But what about warmer climes, you may ask? And aren't there also little cosmetic tips and tricks? Yes, of course. In addition to the usual face cream, we also suggest:

Hand cream and cotton gloves
Hair rollers (woolen scarf optional)
30-year-old, tattered chenille robe
Torn boxer shorts (the perennial favorite)
Ill-fitting T-shirt and men's underwear (women)
Ill-fitting T-shirt and no underwear (men)

"C'MON, SNAP IT UP": 10 THINGS TO SAY TO YOUR SPOUSE DURING SEX

Successfully celibate husbands and wives know there's more to avoiding sex than just being repulsive. Communication is also important—after all, no one can read your mind. You need to talk directly to your partner, telling him or her what's on your mind, especially if you inadvertently find yourselves drifting toward having sex. We make a few suggestions here, but you will want to add your own!

"Gee, was that mole always that color?"
"Do you hear someone downstairs?"
"I think the faucet is dripping."
"C'mon, snap it up."
"Is that a cat fight? Did you let Stuffy out?"
"Hurry up, Terri Garr's on Letterman."
"Is that your *feet*?"
"Oh, did I tell you the mechanic said we need a new clutch?"
"Did you remember to mail in that tax extension?"
"You know where we should go for our vacation?"
"Don't kiss me, I think I'm getting strep throat."

POWER FARTING:
MARITAL BEDTIME ACTIVITIES

And, of course, successfully celibate husbands and wives find time to *share* those special activities that make a marriage so sexless—little things that say "I trust you. I am intimate with you. Get away from me."

In-bed activities fall into several categories. The first would be, traditionally, the *"picking"*:

Picking your nose
Picking your ears
Picking your toes
Picking your belly button
Picking all other areas

Secondly, the *"personal hygiene"*:

Flossing your teeth (flicking used floss most of the way
    off the bed)
Clipping toenails
Clearing your sinuses

Third, the *"personal scratching"*:

Underarms
Crotch

Forth, the *"complement of belches"*:

The "Fanfare"
The "Rolling Surf"

The "Never-ending Story"
The "Miniseries"
The "Chinese Food Re-do"

And finally, of course, the *"Cavalcade of Gas"*:

The "Stealth"
The "Window-breaker"
The "Mattress-burner"
The "Uzi"
The "Rocket-booster"
The "Shy Squeaker"
The "Chili Salute"

Part Six

IF ALL ELSE FAILS, HOW TO RUIN A RELATIONSHIP

So you've gotten yourself enmeshed into a relationship. Marriage, perhaps, or some sort of series of repeated encounters with the same, presumably brain-dead individual.

But even in this seemingly impossible situation, there's still plenty of room for hope—well-tested techniques and strategies for ruining even the most promising relationships.

ELEMENTARY RELATIONSHIP RUINING

Most people find it most useful to pick one strategy and stick to it determinedly. Stubbornly. Mercilessly. Here are some of the most popular (you may want to choose the method best suited to your particular personality):

"The Conversationalist"

Endless discussions of the relationship, preferably working the word "relationship" into as many sentences as possible:
"We need to talk about the relationship."
"I want to know where this relationship is going."

"What do you want from this relationship?"
"Where do *you* think this relationship is going?"

Or, alternatively, use of the word *us*, as in "Honey, I'd like to talk about *us.*"

"The Clam"

The reverse of "The Conversationalist": refusal to discuss the relationship in any way whatsoever; refusal to discuss your feelings, refusal to discuss your lack of feelings, and refusal to discuss your feelings about your refusal to discuss your feelings; also, in its advanced form, refusal to discuss your childhood, your teenagehood, your college years, your morning, your afternoon, your drive home, your plans for the weekend, or what you feel like having for dinner.

"Mr. (or Ms.) Supportive"

Any news of partner's business success or career advancement met with remarks such as:

"You think you're so hot, don't you?"
(Alternatively, news of business setbacks met with "When are you going to give it up?")
Timing your anxiety attacks to coincide with partner's deadlines ("Maybe your deadlines are more important than *we* are.")

DATES TO FORGET

Birthdays
Anniversaries
Valentine's Day
Mother's Day and Father's Day
Christmas
The day you met
The day you first kissed
That romantic evening in that quaint old Vermont inn—wait,
   that was someone else

"The Helpful Questioner"

"Your secretary has the hots for you, doesn't she?"

"She's thinner than me, isn't she?"

"Don't you usually get home at 6:30? It's almost 7. I was worried about you."

"How come you're eating a breath mint? What are you trying to hide?"

"Is your hair wet? Did you take a shower?"

"You never *used* to order paella."

"Why did you bring me flowers? Are you feeling guilty or something?"

"It doesn't take that long to return videos. Were you making phone calls somewhere?"

"How come you're exercising? Trying to look good for someone?"

"Isn't this an awful lot of mileage on your car?"

"Wearing after-shave again. Meet somebody?"

"What do you mean, I look nice? Do I usually look lousy? Who are you comparing me to?"

"The Observant Commentator"

"You won't be happy till you ruin everything."
"You want to see me fail, don't you? Admit it."
"You've never loved me, have you?"
"You just married me to destroy me."

Remember, in ruining a relationship, it's important to remember the little things!

How he was reading *People* while you were in labor.
That time he called you by the wrong name.
How she dented your car and you never said anything about it.
How at first he liked your friend better.
How you still like his friend better.
His friend has a pretty good job.
His friend dresses quite nicely, too.
His friend didn't forget your birthday.

Shared activities can also be very productive—shopping, for example! Hunting for that perfect shade of yarn, assembling fishing supplies, looking for auto parts, winter coats, purses, or doilies are all promising expeditions to force your partner to share with you.

And don't forget those special little conversations one can only truly have in an intimate relationship:

"The Tax Refund"

"Now remember, let's not go crazy with this."
"What, you think I'm stupid? You think I'm out of control? You think I'm a child who can't handle finances?"
"I didn't say that."
"Yes, you did, you said I was crazy! I'm sick and tired of the way you always call me names!"
"I don't always call you names! Although frankly, maybe I should. . . ."

"The Maternal Visit"

"My mother's coming to visit."
"Great! Where's she staying?"

"The 'Okay' Debate"

"Let's have Chinese food."
"Okay."
"What do you mean, 'okay'?"
"I said, 'okay.'"
"No, you didn't. You said 'okay,' as though you were doing me a big favor."
"I did not. I said it like this: 'Okay.'"
"That's not how you said it before."
"That *is* how I said it before."
"No, you said it like this: 'Okay.'"
"I did not say it like that."

And what about responding to your partner's innermost, private thoughts?

Good Responses to Your Partner's Secret Desires

"So you like garters, so what?"

"What do you mean, shave? It's Saturday."

"What do you mean, shower? It's Saturday."

"But I brushed my teeth twelve hours ago. What are you talking about?"

But what about . . . uh, *devices*, you may ask? *You* know, um, battery-controlled "relationship helpers"? Yes, yes, we know what you mean. "Marital toys," as they're sometimes euphemistically called. There's no need to be coy! We all know the primary device you're referring to— of course, *the TV remote control*. You may already be aware of this device and even have privately experimented with it.

Traditionally, of course, it has three primary uses in the context of a committed, serious relationship:

1. *Power struggle over who controls it.* The prime activity; when done skillfully, can take hours, repeatedly, every night of the week.

2. *Obnoxious behavior when obtaining possession.* Usually in one of two forms:

(a) slack-jawed, mindless, incessant changing of channel.

(b) slack-jawed, mindless refusal to change channel away from "Star Search."

3. *Obnoxious behavior when losing possession.* (Also known as the "don't be shy, speak your mind" school of running commentary):

"You've seen this episode of 'CHiPs' about a million times."

"I really don't care about these ocean currents."

"How long are they going to keep playing that goddamn game?"

"I can't believe they gave that woman her own show."

"Don't you want to kill those kids?"

"Oh, please, not the local news, I can't stand that weatherman."

"Wait, wait, I like this commercial."

"What, is that supposed to be funny?"

"What's going on? Who's he?"

"Why do they spell CHiPs that way?"

But what if none of this works? What if, despite repeated exposure to your normal, everyday self, this . . . this *person* is still there? Greeting you at the door, sharing your dinner table, grinning foolishly, even affectionately, at your most disagreeable behavior? Worse, what if you're beginning to enjoy it? The little shared activities, the little private jokes, the special little way she knows just how you like your toast?

ADVANCED RELATIONSHIP RUINING

So, enjoying your toast, are you? You've been having toast and coffee every morning for a while, haven't you? Getting into a bit of a rut, aren't you? Wearing those suits to work, driving the same route, listening to that same radio station . . . oldies, isn't it? Turning into your dad, aren't you? Next thing you know you'll be planting bulbs on Saturday, shopping for furniture, and crashing out in front of the TV, while she and your mother gang up on you

about buying a bigger house, like you can afford this one.
Wasn't the way she just offered you more coffee kind of
pushy? I bet she could turn into one of those real harpies.
Is it stuffy in this room, or are you just suffocating?

There! Feel better?

And if you're the one on the opposite side of the table?
Naturally, use the same technique:

I'm losing myself, aren't I? I don't think about what I
need anymore. I only think about what he wants. Don't we
always do what he wants to do? Planting those bulbs,
looking at those crummy couches, and watching TV.
Sure, everything's what he likes. Now I suppose he wants
some more goddamn coffee. Like I'm supposed to be a
goddamn mind reader. Why am I pouring his coffee? What
am I, his slave? Maybe I should go to one of those
assertiveness classes. Who the hell is he? Screw him and
his bulbs! I'm going to law school.

There. That was simple!

And, of course, in an emergency, there are always the
ultraadvanced techniques. Be careful, these are not for
the amateur, as you can see by this brief comparison:

Elementary R-Ruining	Advanced R-Ruining
Forgetting that cute little story about the tie rack he made for Dad in cub scouts	Forgetting his name
Forgetting where you left his kid's sweater	Forgetting where you left his kid
Sleeping with his T-shirt	Sleeping with his boss

Turning them into a more well-rounded person

Turning them into the IRS

Showing your buddies the dent she made in your fender

Showing your buddies the "naked" videos

Conclusion

MAINTAINING THE ZERO-SEX LIFESTYLE

Well, there it is. You've achieved zero sex. With a little luck, and practice, you should be able to maintain it indefinitely. In fact, you'll probably discover your new habits becoming more and more automatic.

At dinner parties you'll find yourself not even noticing that handsome neurosurgeon or lithe ballerina, but naturally gravitating to the host's parents. Your daydreams at work will center entirely around dinner, you'll walk right by the displays of cosmetics, perfumes, and aftershaves en route to purchasing your new umbrella (or even galoshes), and eventually you won't even want that Ferrari!

But remember, don't be too harsh on yourself if you sometimes have a relapse. Even if you do slip up and have that occasional lifeguard or stewardess, there's no need to punish yourself and go off on a dating binge, or worse, contemplate getting involved in a relationship. Just pick yourself up and get back on track.

Remember, you've already proven you can have zero sex. There's absolutely no reason you can't have it again and for the rest of your life. It's just a matter of knowing your own potential—of having the confidence to believe in yourself. Even if you were born with an enchanting smile, lustrous hair, and taut, sinewy muscle tone, you know you have the power within you to be dull, irritating, sour, and obnoxious. You've done it before. You can do it again. Even the most tolerant, loving human being can be sent screaming into the night.

Yes, you too can finally achieve that secret bliss, the ultimate "oneness of being," the destiny you know has always been yours: the complete zero-sex lifestyle.